I have not been formally diagnosed

Alex Johnston

Presentation by *BookLeaf Publishing*

Web: www.bookleafpub.com

E-mail: info@bookleafpub.com

ISBN: 978-93-95755-64-1

First edition 2022

For Charlotte

ACKNOWLEDGEMENT

I'd like to thank my brain for trying to completely ruin my life at every opportunity but in doing so giving me the ability to create like no other.

PREFACE

This book was a crime of opportunity, talking about your feelings is alot easier when it sounds pretty.

Jarvis

I wear glasses to see
Without them everything would blur
I take them off to look in the mirror
But today I kept them on
And all the flaws I thought were there
Had gone

Adam

Everything in the house is perfect
The table is set
The bed is made
The floors been mopped
The carpets been cleaned
The dishes are done
And the shelves are dusted
So if everything in the house is perfect,
Why am I in it?

Snide Remarks

I've been to many professionals
Looked at under a microscope
I tell them how I feel
They write it down
I tell them horrible things
That keep me awake
I say everything is overwhelming
And I can't go on
But the last one I saw
Told me the worst news of all
I asked for a diagnosis
And he said you have a terrible case
Of being alive

Journal

Back to the old house, what once was mine
An old diary hidden under the mattress
Worn pages with fading text portray old
sentiments
Wishes, pleas, begging
For answers. For help. For death
It was written so long ago, but holds true to this
day
If not more true than when it was first penned
Perhaps even the words knew what was to come
before even I did.

Charlotte

5

Every time I wash the dishes
I turn on the hot water up to scalding levels
It cleans much faster
But when I'm done
I turn on the cold water for just a few seconds
So that if she uses the tap after me
She wont get burned

We dont talk about it

When you go quiet in the group
Become reserved and anxious
We notice

But we dont talk about it

When you come to my place with bloody hands
Hiding them in your sleeves
We see them

But we dont talk about it

Life is a game and the prize is death
When you tried to claim your winnings early
We remember

But we dont talk about it

Within what walls (will I be safe)

I lie in bed at night
Within the walls I grew up in
Surrounded by memories
and I hear them
They come without warning
creeping up on me
They call my name
As if they have any right to use it
In tears I writhe
Fighting them off me as if I could ever break
free
I struggle fruitlessly against myself
Until daylight

I lie in bed at night
Next to my love
Safely encapsulated
by the warmth of a new home
I shut my eyes to rest easy
and I still hear them

Personified

A dream catcher sighs and leans over to breathe
Forlorn and despaired harsh feelings do creep
Another approaches, pray tell whats wrong
My owners dreams are agonising, painful and
long
Well thats what we're for, bad dreams to take
He cries yes that I know but my owners awake

Ouroboros

The stars seem so far when they're painted on
Forced to perceive the lie, against ones own will
Not allowed to decide for yourself when you're
done
Told to believe or die, the irony alone could kill
How am I meant to seperate myself
From myself?
Do you drink the water you know to be poisoned
Trying to quench a thirst safely
When its your only option
What else could I do to escape me?
If both serpents lie
I am bound to be eaten
Trying to trick them is fruitless
And only amounts to treason
Forget reason
Ill touch the moon and be cured
She's waiting for me
Until then I'll avert my gaze
It'll consume me forever
The night sky's Allure

Borrow me with interest

On a bus where the destination is home we are
bound to ride forever
Gripping the support rail as if at any moment I
might be left behind
The eyes of strangers I dare not meet for I
See myself in all of them and I see nothing at all
Blanket stares cover me with the warmth and
fire of the sun
Name me a prophet and ill predict my own end
The powerless seek nothing more than choice
An invitation to the masquerade
A mask formed from apathy
Cracks in the facade drip to the floor
Unable to coalesce with another when others
masks are their truth
And in truth I find I was created without mercy
In truth I am more lost than ever
And if I was created for a purpose
truely it couldn't have been to suffer alone

Prometheus

Eyes carving shapes in the ceiling
Body tensed and ready for a fight that never
comes
Years could pass without even a postcard saying
they left in the first place
Unable to move while every muscle is burning
Get up
Go
No need for clothes, the want of a human
Open the door, silence pouring out of me
Play by the rules
The outside air rushes to be inside of me
Worlds worst hotel with infinite rooms and two
guests to share it
Create the void with the tools I stole
Destroy it as callously as possible for someone
made to love
The air realises the hostility and attacks the
senses
The body plays dead
But to act you must be lying else it become truth
Nothing weighing me down, I will evaporate
soon
And suddenly the years become tangible again
A blade in the sternum, remove it and perish

If screaming were water I'd be the thirstiest man
alive
Thoughts like clay pigeons
Poised to dissolve
Waiting for something to happen
But nothing happens
What did you expect?

Oxazepam

Theres a witch in a hut in a swamp in a lake in a
forest with a roof and a front door painted green
(she loves green) and a black cat named Chance
and he was a human but fell for a trap and the
witch bakes pies when she's lonely sometimes
but the flies eat the pastry or at least they try but
Chance swats them away and purrs as they
dance in the air and did I mention her front door
is green and the steps brick but not the scratchy
kind of brick the smooth one and two plums in
every pie she makes but nothing more she hates
than traversing the lake to take more but to bake
without would be fruitless and moreover the
swamp grows clovers which the witch collects
with a pinch to break the stem and keep the
leaves stop breaking us please the plants plead I
didn't know you could speak she'd breathe and
then she'd leave and put a curse on the plants so
they couldn't feel pain anymore and it's not clear
if this was a mercy but this isn't real and
therefore doesn't matter.

Also Chance turned back into a human whilst
exploring the inside of a hollow log and was

subsequently crushed by the rapid expansion in an enclosed space but he did not suffer long and you shouldn't think about it too hard.

Home

Cursed to roll a stone up the hill forever
Struggle becomes habit becomes comfort
becomes home
never daring climb without it
Fear of your strength if unencumbered
More fear of your weakness displayed
For you are nothing without your burden
Your mistakes and transgressions a mountain
Your stone made to atone
If allowed to walk alone this mountain cannot be
forgiven

Although

You may think me Sisyphus, but I am Atlas in
disguise
But the weight's been growing lighter by the day
A lifelong friend leaving home
Shoulders soft to the touch
I'm scared to be alone
I know not of greener pastures so,
How can I be safe in the unknown?

So thus

It's been a year without the stone
Yet I still climb my last friend
And when I reach the top of that hill
I walk back down again

10 Minute break

I always wished cigarettes lasted longer
They're over too soon
But to have a second is futile, enjoy something
more than you're allowed
And it's sure to turn sour
Time spent with friends is a rush
But burns out all the same
Love is a cigar that is shared
But grows smaller the more its passed
While I inhale you
You exhale me
In the time it takes to finish a cigarette
We've said hello, good morning, and goodbye
And while it was fun
Maybe i'm okay with finishing this smoke

Your only positive impact on the world was when you showed me Joy Division

We met before I was ready
I brought love to your gun fight

You told me you weren't worth it
That was the only time you didn't lie

The antithesis of what I deserved
You shaped me without my permission

I realise now why we're so different
You were bred while I was born

When you tried to go to heaven early
I tied you down with the weight of my youth

You thanked me physically
Unseen scars remain

I held you as you screamed
And i'm ashamed I used force

I don't regret my actions

I just regret yours

I heal more every day
Without you opening my wounds anymore

There's something outside

Im compelled to open the door,
For to really see one must experience
Harm was a certainty I knew was wished upon
me
But maybe for a moment I might catch a glimpse
Just a peek
couldn't hurt
Lying's a sin
The lock clicks shut and the tears begin to well
Turning away is my only choice
If I shut my eyes fact becomes fiction
On the other side must've surely come from hell
Theres more
You don't think
That door was alone
I shudder as the cupboards lay open before me
Shut one shut another they slam as I struggle
The windows laugh with a gaping mouth
I blind them for now until I calm down
You're mistaken
my friend
I'll wait forever
In shadows in sunlight It follows and mocks
Over my shoulder perched just out of sight
It bides it's time not getting bored

I cannot take this anymore

I will open the door on one condition
You promise that when enact your desires on me
I'll be at peace

Waste (time)

I cant find my lighter
I'll count the times I blink a day
And try not to tomorrow
Im going to be late
Forget a year in a second
I wouldn't choose to remember
Maybe its in my jeans
Who chose this for me?
Maybe its in my genes
Must be on the shelf
With photos from when I was fine
Brief moments of respite between hell and
nightmares
Oh, it was in my pocket the whole time

Actuality

23

For I am closed
Resting inert, alone and covert
Inside is where cold is born, lives, and dies
Don't open me please, I wish to preserve
Guard my inner sanctum of frost for whatever its
worth
Empty but for a still beating heart

Originality

A fear of mine
Is rooted in the theory
That no thought is original
Every word or sentence you may speak
Has been spoken before
By someone better, smarter, funnier, more
interesting
And it makes me wonder
If nothing I create
Is truly mine
What if i'm not the first me?

Nostalgia

25

It's impossible to be perfect
I wear a different face wherever I go
So that I may appeal to the most people
I desire to be remembered without my flaws
To be put on a pedestal and fondly thought of
But to be known is to be criticised
And It does not sit well with me that I am not
idealised
Like nostalgia
So sometimes I think
I would be happier as a memory

Gifted child

You're gifted
That mind belongs to an adult
Your potential is unimaginable and incalculable
Programs for the unique
We'll nurture your talent

You're average
That mind is definitely yours
Your potential is a choice and something to aim
for
Programs for the masses
We'll support your endeavours

You're a failure
That mind is wasted on you
Your potential was not reached and misguided
Programs to fix you
We'll try to forget you